The Decorative Christmas

The Decorative Christmas

Jeannie Walker

Cape Town

This book is dedicated to all born hoarders who
will have most of the materials required in boxes
and drawers somewhere around their homes, and
to many enthusiastic and helpful friends: Alex,
Betty, Gretchen, Norma, Janetta, Sophie, Pat,
Faith, Margie, Nanette, Karl and Adelaide.

Cover design by Abie Fakier
Photography by David Briers
Styling by Danielle Boschi and Rayne Stroebel
Set in 11/12 pt Souvenir Medium by Studiographix, Cape Town
Printed and bound by National Book Printers, Goodwood
First edition 1989

© 1989 Delos, 40 Heerengracht, Cape Town

ISBN 1-86826-050-X

Contents

Introduction

The religious festival known as the Nativity, the Birth of Jesus Christ or Christmas, was celebrated as a unique event by the early Christian Church in Rome since the middle of the fourth century AD. The choice of the 25th of December as the date for Christmas has puzzled many historians and theologians. Mid-December marks the middle of winter in Europe, and it coincides with a number of pagan festivals held at this same early period.

In discussing the Christmas event, historians have noted the manner in which ancient pagan festivals have moulded the traditions and celebrations which we observe at present. This is seen in numerous practices: the use of evergreen vegetation such as the Christmas tree and the wreath at the door, the giving of presents, the lighting of candles, and generally a time for parties which mark the end of the old year and the beginning of the new.

Actually, many of the colourful ornamentations which we associate with Christmas have a much shorter history. Within the last century and a half the Christmas tree has been decorated with biscuits and sweets, toys, electric fairy lights and the like. Christmas cards were designed in the 1840s and were sent everywhere around the world. Christmas gifts, which in times past were regarded simply as an act of charity, have been extended in numerous ways. It is no longer merely an exchange of gifts among family and friends – nowadays employees expect an annual bonus cheque.

In South Africa, our manner of celebrating Christmas is greatly influenced by what we have absorbed from practices of the nations in the Northern Hemisphere. Germans, Swedes, English and Americans, among others, have passed on traditions which we have made our own, although there have been some changes mainly to give them a South African character. Thus, under a blazing mid-summer December sun, a main Christmas meal generally includes cold roast turkey, Christmas pudding and mince pies with ice cream - like the fare that is enjoyed in European and American homes in their cold climate in mid-winter.

It is therefore intriguing to ponder over the extent to which ancient customs have been imposed upon our Christmas traditions, and on how much has been borrowed from European Christmas festivals in making the Christmas season the occasion which we enjoy today.

In choosing the 25th of December for one of the early Church's most significant celebrations, the Church Fathers moulded the festival out of the many Roman festivals that were taking place around them at the same time. Thus, with the Saturnalia the Romans were honouring a past Golden Age and were hoping for its return. The feast of Brumalia marked the birth of the unconquered sun, and the Kalendar Januarii was a New Year's feast.

This symbolic reference to light, renewal and rebirth, was a significant feature of the New Church. Rather than condemning the past, the Church enveloped it and allowed it to influence the mode of Christian worship.

The use of evergreen plants and flowers to decorate churches and homes at Christmas time was adopted from a Roman tradition: during midwinter a gift of a sprig of an evergreen tree was a token of good luck. The Christian Church in Rome found praiseworthy qualities in certain plants, such as the holly. The symbolic features which they identified with the life of Christ were the sharp pointed leaves, while they felt the blood-red berries represented the crown of thorns.

Wreaths at Advent time are associated with the Swedish Saint Lucia. The legendary Saint dated from a time before Christianity was widely accepted in Sweden. St Lucia, wealthy by birth, was praised for her deep concern for the poor, for she gave all that she had to feed and clothe the destitute. As a young woman she was admired for her beliefs and practices as a Christian. The Crown of Lights is a symbol of her halo. Traditionally, the crown is covered in evergreen boughs and holds four candles. One candle is lit on each of the four Advent Sundays (which generally commence on the last Sunday in November).

Before the days of gas and electricity, the only means of lighting dark spaces were oil lamps and candles. The wide use of candles in religious and social events still creates an atmosphere of mystery, sincerity and tranquility. For these qualities a flame was used long before Christians appreciated its significance in that Christ is called the "Light of the World". Some commentators believe that the Jewish festival Hanukkah, "the feast of lights", was adopted by the early Christian Church, since the times of the two festivals almost coincide.

The kissing bunch is associated with an ancient folk festival in England. This elaborate hanging of green leaves is given a contemporary significance by attaching to it red apples, white paper flowers, and dolls representing Mary, Joseph and the infant Jesus. In England, mistletoe – a parasitic plant with white berries – was added to the bunch. Under it couples kissed, with the young man plucking off a berry each time a kiss was exacted. When all the berries had been removed there was no longer a reason to kiss beneath it. Some suspect that this custom belonged to the Druids, a pagan religious group living in England before Christianity. The Druids believed that mistletoe could work miracles of healing and fertility when hung in the homes of their followers.

The Christmas or fir tree was used by early Germanic tribes in their winter celebrations. This is probably the reason why Martin Luther (16th century) is given credit for creating the first Christmas tree. Tradition has it that on a particularly frosty Christmas Eve Luther noticed not only the clearness of the stars in the heavens, but also the fact that fir trees sparkled in the light of the moon. His thoughts turned to the Birth of Christ, and upon reaching home he tried to recreate the vision he had seen, and he used candles to represent the stars.

In England the earliest Christmas trees date from 1829. About a decade later Prince Albert of Saxe-Coberg and Queen Victoria were given credit for popularising the tradition of the Christmas tree, and of making the celebration a British family event. The tree in the palace was decorated with candles, baskets of sweets and fancy cakes. At the base there were sweets, toys and dolls for the royal children.

During the last four centuries the decoration of the Christmas tree has altered according to religious influences, taste, and economic and social circumstances. In the 16th and 17th centuries in Germany the Christmas tree was decorated with Communion wafers and shiny red apples, indicating the religious significance of the festival. In the last century, the ornaments used have changed from hand-made to manufactured, with local and foreign decorations filling the shops many weeks before Christmas. Today the decorations are a personal expression of ingenuity, hand craft, dexterity and individual interest.

The earliest records of the giving of presents is attributed to the ancient Romans, who presented gifts to each other at New Year. The gifts exchanged were mainly honey, cakes and branches of evergreen trees. The exchange of presents on particular anniversaries occurred in pre-Roman times. In the Jewish Feast of Purim, dating from the time of Queen Esther and Mordecai's deliverance of the Jews, the celebration was a time of gladness, feasting and presenting gifts. The giving of presents at Christmas may partly stem from the Magi who brought presents to the Christ Child on the 6th of January or 'Twelfth Night'. A further Christian legend concerns St Nicolas and St Martin, whose feast days occur close to Christmas. Both were associated with giving presents to young children. In the Middle Ages the kind of gifts children received were cakes, apples, nuts, dolls and small toys. St Nicolas (Santa Claus or Father Christmas), is still an important figure at Christmas, yet the range of gifts that children expect and receive today is regulated by their environment and family circumstances.

The Christmas cracker was first devised in the 1850s. The earliest ones were made in France. A cracker included a bag of sweets enclosed in strong paper which had to be pulled apart to expose the contents. An English manufacturer adopted the French idea and enclosed a minute exploding device which was activated the moment when the two parts were pulled apart. At this time sweets were no longer used as a filling, and paper hats, mottoes, riddles and miniature toys were enclosed instead. By 1900 the making of Christmas crackers was described as a minor industry. Few festive parties are without crackers today.

Getting ready for Christmas and New Year involves many activities, preparing menus, making gifts, cards, decorations for the home, seeing friends and family members, and attending carol and church services. One writer recorded his impressions of an American Christmas by emphasising the involvement of the whole family in saving money, baking, sewing, cutting and pasting to celebrate the generous days of Christmas with gifts.

This record of the background behind our customs has been given to indicate the traditions in making Christmas a unique event as we celebrate it at present.

1
Requirements

You will be one of two groups of people: a hoarder or a non-hoarder. The hoarder is one who "squirrels" away all kinds of potentially useful small and large things such as nails, rubber bands, paperclips, coloured paper, old cards, bows, ribbons and string, indeed, all manner of things, knowing that one day they might come in useful. This collector group of readers will find suggestions in *The Decorative Christmas* to be a practicable guide, because most of the requirements listed will be within reach somewhere in their homes. The non-hoarders, however, might face the disadvantage of having to purchase many of the requirements. For both groups some items will be readily available, starting in your kitchen and ending in your storeroom or garage. Once you have looked through the list given below you will be surprised to how easy it will be to make your Christmas festivities more colourful.

Inevitably many items will not be found in your home. Crêpe paper in a variety of colours should be obtainable from a supermarket or news agency, while florist's wire and foam (oasis) can be bought from a hardware shop. Should you live in a small country town, explore what is kept by the shopkeepers in your area. A supplier who is willing to operate a mail order service for listed items is suggested at the back of the book.

After you have looked at the photographs and read the text from Chapters 2 to 8, I hope it will be clear that the level of skill needed, is minimal. The suggestions are generally aimed at older children, who will need parental assistance at times. The measure of skill required, is indicated by the use of stars – one star being the most elementary, with added stars indicating that greater dexterity is involved. The time taken to complete items is suggested by the use of clocks. One clock suggests an hour, while a higher number indicates appropriately longer periods. Actually, some decorations can take days, such as occurs with drying procedures which are slow, or when the number of activities necessary to complete the item is large, as seen in the green fabric wreath with salt ceramic trims.

The Decorative Christmas is presented as a guide, and I hope you will be encouraged to substitute items with what is available in your own area if you cannot find those suggested in this book. This applies mainly to flowers and leaves, fresh and dried, and the availability of fir-cones, which you could substitute with large pods of certain trees. Only a limited number of decorations are described. However, I hope that by looking at the photographs your own creative abilities will be aroused and you will be encouraged to design some decorations yourself.

To make planning easier from the outset, the most common necessities are listed under the locality within the home where they might generally be found.

The kitchen

Irrespective of the size of your kitchen cupboards, you will have essential cooking ingredients such as flour and salt for making salt ceramic hearts and stars. You will also have ingredients for ginger biscuits. (Both these items are mentioned in the chapter on Christmas tree trims.) From your cleaning cupboard you can use household bleach for decorating wrapping paper and Christmas cards. Small and large containers are useful for putting some of your table decorations into. Should you fear that their colour is unsuitable, you can cover them with aluminium foil so as to give them a Christmas sparkle. For this, see Chapters 2 and 8 on Advent wreaths and table decorations. Inexpensive black garbage bags and red and green shelf-paper are easily overlooked. Yet you can give your gifts an unusual, but festive appearance when you use them as wrapping materials. Refer to the chapter on wrapping gifts for detailed information.

The tool box

The most important items obtainable from the tool box are a pair of pliers and a sharp craft knife. Apart from cutting wire with the pliers, they are useful for twisting florist's wire into "stems" – see the spherical Christmas tree. A craft knife with a sharp blade is essential for cutting cardboard and cartridge paper. Keep this tool out of reach of small children.

The sewing box

Most homes have rudimentary requirements for sewing, such as scissors, needles, pins and sewing cottons. The coloured cottons used are red, green,

yellow and white. A sewing machine will make stitching quicker, especially if you are going to make the quilted Christmas tree and the Christmas tree trims: the angel, heart, dove and bell.

An assortment of fabrics in reds and greens from your rag-bag will be valuable for making the fabric wreaths and the patchwork Christmas tree. Larger lengths of fabric, ideally in red, will be necessary for making bows. Many of the red bows seen in the photographs are made from red satin-taffeta torn into 3cm widths. To do this is much cheaper than buying metres of red ribbon. Synthetic florist's ribbon is a suitable substitute.

The games box

Not every family has an enthusiastic table-tennis player. Perhaps you know of someone who is, and who will let you have the discarded ping-pong balls. Painted and varnished they make a colourful and robust substitute for the beautiful fine glass Christmas baubles that are known, alas, for their fragility.

The writing desk

Readily available in most homes are pencils, paperclips, rubbers, a ruler or measuring tape, and a pair of scissors for cutting paper. Schoolgoing children will have a compass and protractor for drawing and dividing a circle. Apart from fluid or quick-drying glues, transparent and double-sided sticking tapes are extremely useful as their sticking properties act immediately.

Poster-paint in red and gold and a quick-drying varnish are required for colouring the ping-pong balls. A small to medium-sized paintbrush will be sufficient for all the painting needs in this book. Be sure to wash the brush well with household soap after applying each colour and varnish.

Throughout the book papers of various thickness are extensively employed. Crêpe paper in red, green, white and pink is used for making the paper roses, Advent wreath, spherical Christmas tree and German Lichtstock. Cartridge paper in white and in a variety of colours is used for the Christmas cards, while thin white paper is used for making decorated wrapping paper. A sheet or two of tracing paper will be useful for tracing templates off the designs provided.

The storeroom

More often than not one forgets about materials stored in a storeroom – until a "clear-out" is organised. I hope your storeroom contains discarded cardboard packing cases, dry-cleaner's wire hangers, bundles of ruined pantihose and odd lengths of string. All of these are useful and you will be glad that you have them.

The above list does not include the more specialist requirements for each decoration. These are listed in the appropriate sections.

The Decorative Christmas with its photographs, diagrams and other information endeavours to help you to make your own family Christmas celebrations visually rich with colourful ornamentation, so that everyone sharing the event will remember it with true appreciation.

2
The Advent Wreath

Advent wreath in green fabric bows

Time: *Skill:* ★

Requirements
Cardboard disc cut from a discarded packing-case
One pair of ruined pantihose
Synthetic wadding, or cut-up pantihose
Green fabric, about 30cm wide
Needle, sewing cotton, scissors
Ruler, compass, pencil, medium-sized paintbrush, poster-paint, varnish
Eight ping-pong balls painted red and gold and varnished
Four red candles
Bowl or dish of your choice
Red ribbon

Method
Measure the diameter of your dish or bowl and cut a cardboard disc to fit.
From the centre of the disc measure 3cm in four directions and cut holes large enough to hold the candles.
Pierce the cardboard about 3cm from the outer edge at intervals to allow you to bind the stuffed pantihose tube to the disc.
Fill a leg of the pantihose or stocking with synthetic wadding until it has the feel of a loose "sausage".
Make the green bows according to the instructions on page 25.
Refer to page 26 for handling the ping-pong balls.
Tie the varnished ping-pong balls in between the "leaves" with thread or string.
Place the candles in the holes.
Drop a length of red ribbon into the centre to add more colour.
Varnished fir-cones or large seed-heads can be added for extra interest around the edge of the dish.

Advent arrangement of paper roses

Time: ⏰ ⏰ ⏰ *Skill:* ★

Requirements

Cardboard disc cut from a discarded packing case
Ruler, pencil, compass
Crêpe paper roses (see instructions opposite)
Scissors
Florist's wire, string
Small blocks of flower foam (oasis)
Four candles
Bowl or dish of your choice

Method

Measure the diameter of your dish and cut a disc of cardboard to fit.

Diagram for the construction of paper roses

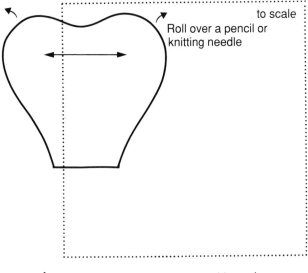

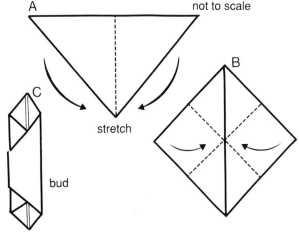

From the centre of the disc measure 3cm in four directions and cut holes large enough to hold the candles.
Pierce the cardboard and tie the four small to medium-sized blocks of flower foam as close to the candles as possible with the string.
Make a sufficient number of roses to fill the bowl. Bear in mind that crêpe paper fades so do not leave it in direct sunlight.
Arrange the roses around the bowl.
Place the candles in the holes.

Paper roses

Time: About three to four can be made in one hour.
Skill: ★ ★

Requirements

Crêpe paper. Red, white, pink and green is used in the illustration, and dyed yellow and orange for extra effect.
Florist's wire
Double-sided sticking tape
One knitting needle of medium thickness
Scissors

Method

Cut out the template from the diagram.
Cut out even petals and a square measuring 5cm x 5cm, making certain that the "crêpe" runs from top to bottom.
Fold the square in half and bring the two outer corners to the lower point and press down.
Next, bring the two outer corners to the centre and roll into a bud shape.
Gently roll the top edges of each petal over the knitting needle between your finger and thumb.
With your forefingers and thumbs stretch the body of the petals.
Create a small tuck in the lower part of each petal and place them one next to the other around the bud.
Wrap a length of florist's wire around the base of the rose and use the remainder as a stem.
With a thin strip of double-sided sticking tape placed in the centre of a thin strip (about 1cm) of green crêpe paper, wrap it around the base of the rose and down the stem.

Tip: Perhaps you do not have any dyes in your home. Try placing 6cm strips of pink, white and red crêpe paper one on top of the other wrapped into a wad and dipped rapidly into water; the dyes of the paper will run and affect all three layers. Dry carefully away from any surface that may get stained by the dye.

Advent arrangement of pink fabric roses

Time: 🕐 🕐 🕐 *Skill:* ★

Requirements

Cardboard for the foundation disc (from a discarded packing case)
Silver foil, clear cellophane
Pink synthetic fabric (lining) 45cm wide
Needle, sewing cotton, scissors, pins
Ruler, pencil, compass
Florist's wire
Green crêpe paper
Double-sided sticking tape, adhesive putty, transparent sticking tape
Sweets with pink wrapping paper
Four pink candles
Bowl or dish of your choice

Method

Measure the diameter of your bowl or dish and cut a disc to fit snuggly inside the rim.
From the centre of the disc measure 3cm in each direction and cut circular holes in it wide enough to hold the candles.
Wrap silver foil around the disc.

Diagram for the construction of fabric roses

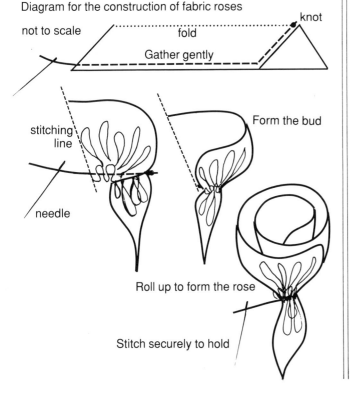

To make the fabric roses cut eight strips 10cm wide on the cross (diagonal or bias) of the fabric.
Fold and pin the edges together.
With a double thread gather the fabric, starting on the visible diagonal edge as in the diagram.
Gather slightly and form a bud by rolling the fabric tightly at first, while at the same time wrapping and gathering the fabric around this basic core. The length allows for this to be done about three times.
Stitch the base together to prevent unravelling.
Form a short loop in the florist's wire and poke the opposite end into the rose.
Cut a short strip of green crêpe paper, about 1,5cm wide, and place a thinner strip of double-sided sticking tape down the centre. Wrap this around the base of the rose and down the wire stem.
Arrange the eight roses around the four candles by piercing the stems through the cardboard and pasting the stems to the lower surface with transparent sticking tape.
The area between the candles is filled by using a 10cm strip of cellophane and thin pliable silver foil. Both are separately folded in half, fringed and gathered, using a needle and thread.
The cellophane is wrapped around the foil and placed into a small mound of adhesive putty.
The sweets are arranged around the roses. Hopefully they will remain there until Twelfth Night!

Advent arrangement of fir-cones and "poinsettias"

Time: 🕐 🕐 🕐 *Skill:* ★

Requirements

Cardboard for a disc from a discarded packing case
Large number of varnished fir-cones
Green crêpe paper, florist's wire
One metre of red florist's ribbon
Thin yellow plastic from a supermarket carrier bag
Transparent sticking tape, double-sided sticking tape, adhesive putty
Ribbon for the bows
Four red candles
Scissors, ruler, compass, pencil, tracing paper

Method

Measure the diameter of your bowl, and cut a disc to fit snuggly inside the rim.

From the centre of the disc measure 3cm in each direction and cut holes in it large enough to hold the candles.

To make the "poinsettias"

Trace the shape of the petal with the tracing paper and cut five petals for each flower from the red florist's ribbon.

Place one end of the florist's wire – about 15cm in length – down the centre of the petal, and stick it down with transparent sticking tape. Trim the transparent tape. Treat each petal in the same manner.

The florettes in the centre of the poinsettias are made by cutting strips of yellow plastic about 1,5cm wide, and placing an even thinner strip of double-sided sticking tape down the centre of the plastic. Wind this around a short length, about 5cm, of florist's wire.

With the florettes and petals firmly in your hand, twist the free ends of wire together to form a stem.

The greenery is made by winding thin strips of green crêpe paper around your hand and binding it in the middle with a length of florist's wire about 15cm in length. Twist this into a stem and poke it among the fir-cones or into the cardboard.

The arrangement is completed by arranging the poinsettias between the fir-cones and adding a bow.

Place the candles in the holes.

Diagram for shape and construction of a poinsettia leaf

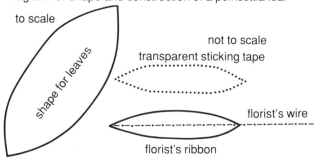

to scale

shape for leaves

not to scale

transparent sticking tape

florist's wire

florist's ribbon

Straw Advent wreath

Time:  *Skill:* ★

Requirements
A substantial handful of long straw, or straw-like grass
Yellow string for binding purposes (Dye the string in tea.)
25cm red fabric, or seven metres of satin or taffeta ribbon
Salt ceramic hearts, painted red
Scissors, needle and red sewing cotton

Method
To make the straw pliable, soak it overnight.
Plait the straw into an even length by adding small quantities of straw as you proceed. This can be as long as you choose, depending on the size of ring required. Unevenness can be camouflaged by decoration.
Form it into a ring by interweaving the ends into the top of the plait.
Trim away excess grass.
Tear or cut the red fabric into 3cm strips. Four lengths are used for hanging purposes and the remainder for bows.
Attach the long strands with needle and thread and tie on the bows.
Decorate with salt ceramic hearts (refer to page 39 for instructions) or any way you choose.

The kissing bunch

Time: ⏰ ⏰ *Skill:* ★

Requirements
Wide mesh chicken wire about 60cm x 30cm
Two blocks of flower foam, or re-use old foam (oasis)
Florist's wire
Green and white crêpe paper
Varnished pods
About ten ping-pong balls painted red and varnished
12cm red fabric cut into 3cm strips for hanging, and for bows for decoration
Four small bells
Dried leaves of your choice

Method
Mould the chicken wire into a spherical shape.
Before you close it, insert the flower foam, cut into smaller pieces.

Make a loop with wire at the top and base of the sphere for attaching the ribbons.
Make white paper roses (refer to page 16 for instructions).
For adding tabs to ping-pong balls, refer to page 26 for instructions.
If the pods lack stems, add tabs to them in the same manner as the ping-pong balls, and make stems with florist's wire.
To make the "filling" greenery, cut strips of green crêpe paper about 2cm wide and 40cm long – wind each strip around your hand, grasp the centre point and twist. Bind the "bow" with a length of florist's wire bent double. Twist the ends together to form a stem. A large number of "bows" are required to go around the kissing bunch.
Insert the roses, pods, bows and dried leaves into the foam and fill the gaps with the crêpe paper greenery.
Attach the ribbons to the top and bottom loops.
Tie the bells to the lower loop.

3
The Wreath
for the Door

Christmas wreath in colourful fabrics

Time:  *Skill:* ★

Requirements

One wire coat-hanger
One pair of ruined pantihose
10cm x 150cm strip of synthetic wadding (alternatively several cut-up pantihose)
Fabric from the rag-bag, in yellow, red, green, blue and orange for bows
Needles, scissors, sewing cotton
Strip of red fabric for a large bow

Method

Manipulate the coat-hanger into a ring.
Stuff the pantihose with wadding (or alternative); wind this around the hanger and secure with stitching. Any lumps may be moulded by twisting the string around the frame.
To make the bows, cut the coloured fabric into strips 4cm x 17cm.

For each bow, bring both ends to the centre with a slight overlap.
Stitch the three layers together, pull tight, and twist the thread two or three times around the stitching line to form a bow.
Stitch to the wreath. About sixty bows are required for the wreath in the illustration.
Finally add the red bow.

Diagram for constructing fabric bows

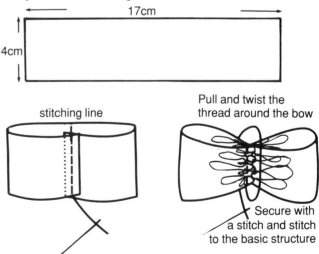

Green wreath with salt ceramic heart and stars

Time:  Skill:

Requirements
One wire coat-hanger
One pair of ruined pantihose
10cm x 150cm strip of synthetic wadding
(alternative stuffing made of cut-up pantihose)
Green fabric for approximately sixty bows
Red strip of fabric for larger bow
Needle, green sewing cotton, scissors
Stars and hearts (refer to page 39 for instructions)

Method
Manipulate the coat-hanger into a ring.
Stuff the pantihose with wadding (or alternative); wind this around the hanger and secure with stitching. Any lumps may be moulded by twisting string around the frame.
To make the bows, cut the green fabric into strips of 4cm x 16cm.
Bring the ends to the centre with a slight overlap.
Stitch the three layers together, pull tight, and twist the thread twice or three times around the stitching line to form a bow.

Stitch to the wreath.
Add the red bow at the top and tie the hearts and stars to the ring.

Wreath of dried cones, nuts, leaves, and painted ping-pong balls

Time: Skill: ★ ★

Requirements
One wire coat-hanger
Thin florist's wire
Three pairs of ruined pantihose
Four to five ping-pong balls
Red poster paint, varnish
Two pieces of thin silver foil (teabag wrappers)
Medium paintbrushes
Small quantity of soft fabric cut into 0,5cm x 1,5cm strips
Glue
Wire paperclips
About twelve pecan nuts
About four small fir-cones
Small twigs of dried leaves
A strip of fabric for a bow, or florist's ribbon
Scissors, pliers

Method
Manipulate the hanger into a ring.
Cut away the body part of the pantihose and

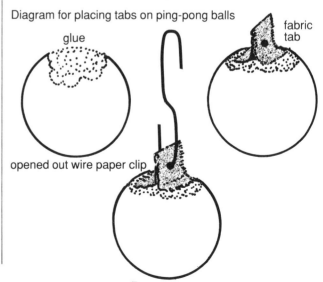

Diagram for placing tabs on ping-pong balls

26

tightly plait the "legs" around the wire frame; the idea is to allow you to thread the stems of the twigs in and out of the plait, thereby securing them without using too much florist's wire.

Glue a strip of fabric to the ping-pong balls (diagram), and allow to dry.

Pierce a small hole through the fabric and thread the item to a pulled-out "S"-shaped paper clip – this enables you to hold the object while painting or varnishing it. Paint the ping-pong balls red and then varnish them and the nuts; hang them to dry. Varnish the fir-cones or other pods of your choice. When the varnish is dry – this might take one or two days – attach florist's wire to the ping-pong balls through the fabric tabs.

Work through three nuts at a time (this will give you four bunches), around the base of the fir-cones.

Place these with the vegetation around the ring.

Intersperse with four rosettes of thin silver foil made from half the teabag wrapping, gathered along one edge, fringed, drawn-up and tied.

Decorate with one or two bows in the position of your choice.

Dried flower wreath

Time: Skill:

Requirements

Dried flowers from your garden

Start a week in advance by picking the vegetation of your choice and hanging it upside-down in a warm area. Each region of the country differs climatically, so it is best not to specify the kind of vegetation.

One wire coat-hanger

Thinnest florist's wire available

Three pairs of ruined pantihose

Paper roses for extra colour, crêpe paper in the colour of your choice, also green for the stems

Double-sided sticking tape

Scissors, pliers for cutting the wire

Bows of fabric ribbon, crêpe paper and synthetic florist's ribbon

Method

Manipulate the hanger into a ring.

Cut away the body part of the pantihose and plait the legs tightly around the wire frame; the idea is

to allow you to thread the stems of the vegetation in and out of the plait, thereby securing them without using too much florist's wire.

Place the vegetation evenly around the ring.

Should there be areas requiring extra colour you wish to fill in with paper roses, refer to page 16 for instructions.

Complete the wreath by adding a bow or bows at the base of the ring.

Wreath of leaves

Time:  Skill: ★

Requirements
Twigs of leaves from an evergreen bush
One wire coat-hanger
Thinnest florist's wire available
Three pairs of ruined pantihose
Scissors, needle, sewing cotton, pliers
Several lengths of synthetic florist's ribbon, about three metres long in the colours of your choice. (Red, blue, green, yellow, orange and purple are used for the wreath in the photograph.)

Method
Manipulate the hanger into a ring.
Cut away the body part of the pantihose and plait the legs tightly around the wire frame; the idea is to allow you to thread the stems of the leaves in and out of the plait, thereby securing them without using too much florist's wire.
Place the leaves evenly around the ring.
Complete the wreath by winding the synthetic florist's ribbon around the wreath, allowing the long ends to hang down.

Wreath of fresh flowers

Time: 🕐 🕐 *Skill:* ★

Requirements

Fresh flowers and leaves from your garden
One wire coat-hanger
Thinnest florist's wire available
Three pairs of ruined pantihose
Scissors, needle, sewing cotton, pliers
Bow of fabric or of florist's synthetic ribbon

Method

Manipulate the coat-hanger into a ring.
Cut away the body part of the pantihose and plait the legs tightly around the wire frame. The idea is to allow you to thread the stems in and out of the plait, thereby securing them without using too much florist's wire.
Arrange the flowers and leaves evenly around the ring, using the florist's wire where necessary.
Complete the wreath by adding a bow either to the top or to the base.
Frequently spray with water to keep the flowers and leaves fresh.

4
The Christmas Tree

The conventional Christmas tree

The conventional Christmas tree is a universal delight; for the purist there is no substitute for it.

German Lichtstock

Time:  *Skill:*

Requirements
Cardboard (a large discarded cardboard box)
Cardboard tube discarded from a fabric shop, or made with cardboard
Green and red crêpe paper
$\frac{1}{2}$ metre red taffeta for the ribbons and bows, to be torn into 3cm strips
 Scissors, sharp craft knife

Strip of corrugated cardboard (2-ply) about 5cm wide and three metres long (This is more flexible than packing-case cardboard.)
String, glue, needle, red sewing cotton

Method
Cut out three rings from the cardboard:
1   Diameter 55cm x 4cm
2   Diameter 42cm x 4cm
3   Diameter 29cm x 4cm
Keep the central disc for the base.
Roll the two-ply corrugated cardboard around one end of the tube and glue together. Stitch the coil to the base (see diagram).
Cover with green crêpe paper.
Wind green and red strips of crêpe paper around the tube and secure with glue at both ends. Tie a green bow at the base of the tube.
Wrap a strip of green crêpe paper 4cm wide around each circular frame, and once again with fringed twisted green crêpe paper 6cm wide (use double pieces of paper).
Tear ten strips of fabric 3cm wide. Stitch strips at even intervals to the largest circle.
For the middle-sized circle, the strips should be

The use of candles

Flickering candles add a magical quality of their own to the Christmas environment and are a very necessary accessory. If you are going to light the candles, make sure you have a FIRE EXTINGUISHER nearby to protect yourself and your home. IMPORTANT – do not blow the candles out too vigorously as you might blow the flame towards the paper. GREAT CARE MUST BE EXERCISED AT ALL TIMES WHEN THE CANDLES ARE ALIGHT. KEEP CHILDREN AWAY FROM OPEN FLAMES. Extinguish with wet cotton wool held to the wick.

Spherical Christmas tree

Time: 🕐 🕐 🕐 Skill: ★ ★ ★

Requirements
Cardboard (medium-size discarded cardboard box)
Wide chicken-wire mesh.
Cardboard tube (discarded from a fabric shop or made up)
Green and red crêpe paper (about six to seven packets of green to cover the sphere)
Florist's wire
Pliers
Scissors
Compass, pencil, ruler
Medium-size box or flower pot in which to stand the tree

Diagram for the construction of the spherical Christmas tree

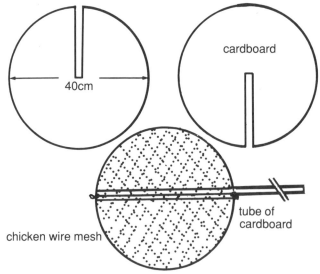

about 53cm in length; and for the small circle the strips should be about 24cm long.
Tear further strips to make bows to place at the base of the hanging ribbons.
Make bows to tie at intervals on the largest circular frame.
Stitch the four lengths of ribbon together at right angles so that they hang across the top of the tube. Place another bow on the top of the three layers of ribbons.
Decorate with salt ceramic hearts and ginger biscuits (refer to page 39).

Method

Cut two discs 40cm in diameter, and interlock them as in the diagram.

This forms the frame around which to wrap the wire to make a sphere.

Wrap the chicken-wire around the framework. Pinch the top and bottom edges together and secure with wire.

Place the tube in the sphere and wire to the tip and cardboard framework.

Cut numerous 14cm diameter circles (use a saucer as a template) from the green crêpe paper.

Place two together. Fold the circle into quarters, hold the base and twist the lower 1cm between your finger and thumb (diagram).

Wrap a piece of florist's wire around this section, twist together and wrap around the mesh of the chicken-wire.

Cover the tree in this manner.

Decorate with red and gold painted and varnished ping-pong balls, or in a manner of your choice (for treatment of ping-pong balls see page 26).

Decorate the tube with strips of red and green crêpe paper, and tie a bow at the base after having secured it in the container.

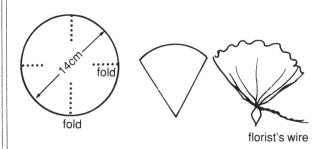

florist's wire

33

secure the green and red fabric and/or paper to the sides of the cardboard shapes.

Neaten the edges with a strip of crêpe paper 6cm wide and folded in half, and glue to both sides of the edge.

Slot the one half of the Christmas tree into the other.

Balance or secure by glueing the tree to the covered box.

Trimmings can be held to the tree by sticking dressmaker's pins into the cardboard.

Diagram for the construction of the patchwork Christmas tree

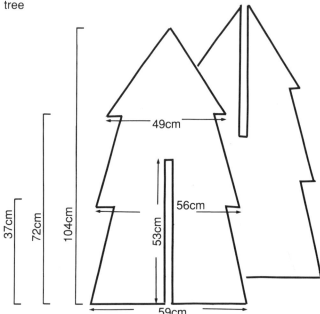

Patchwork Christmas tree

Time: 🕐 🕐 🕐   Skill: ★ ★ ★

Requirements

One large corrugated cardboard packing case; dimensions required 2cm x 104cm x 60cm
Scraps of red and green fabric, and paper
Green crêpe paper
Double-sided sticking tape, glue
Scissors, a sharp craft knife, pins
A medium-sized box covered with green crêpe paper for support and a bow of green crêpe paper
Golden bow (optional)

Method

Follow the measurements in the diagram for the shape of the tree.
Cut out two with the sharp craft knife.
With either the glue or double-sided sticking tape

Fabric (quilted) Christmas tree

Time: 🕐 🕐 🕐   Skill: ★ ★

Requirements

Green fabric, approximately 115cm x 140cm
Synthetic wadding, approximately 115cm x 75cm
Scraps of red fabric
Green and red stitching cotton, tacking cotton
Needle, pins, scissors, sewing-machine (optional)
Newspaper, pencil
One wire coat-hanger
Yellow fabric for the star, brass beads, yellow ribbon, and four small bells

Place manipulated coat-hanger into the opening and stitch together.

Cover the hook with a tube of yellow fabric.

Make a star from fabric and decorate with beads, the bow and the bells (refer to page 41 for the pattern of the star).

Diagram for the construction of the quilted Christmas tree

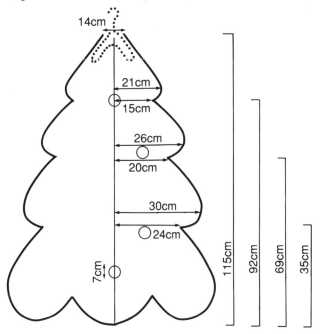

14cm

21cm

15cm

26cm

20cm

30cm

24cm

7cm

115cm

92cm

69cm

35cm

Method

Enlarge the diagram on newspaper to fit the dimensions of the fabric.

Cut out.

Place the pattern on the double-folded fabric and cut out.

Tack the wadding to one shape and trim.

Cut six circles in red fabric and stitch to the other green shape.

Place ready for stitching on the sewing machine:

1 wadding

2 green fabric

3 second layer of green fabric with red "baubles", the right side facing the first piece of green fabric.

Stitch around the perimeter, allowing 1,5cm margin and leaving the top of the tree free.

Snip around the edge, especially in all the angles.

Turn inside out carefully.

Stitch around each bauble in order to secure the wadding. Pull out tacking threads.

35

5
The Christmas Tree Trims

Paper stars

Time:  *Skill:* ★

Requirements
Stiff cartridge paper
Sharp craft knife
Glue, or hand-cut thin strips of double-sided sticking tape
Thread to hang

Method
First of all, for each of the stars, cut strips of paper about 3mm to 4mm wide

Star A

24cm x 8cm lengths (twelve for the inner ring and twelve for the outer ring)
12cm x 6cm lengths for the added loop in the outer ring.
Place dabs of glue or small squares of double-sided sticking tape on all the ends of the paper strips.
Form these into single and double loops.

Glue twelve loops into a ring, following the diagram to form the inner circle.
Place dabs of glue at the base of the double loops and stick to the inner circle.
Hang by a thread through one of the loops.

Star B

For the central ring, a strip of paper 29cm long
For the outer ring of double loops:
8cm x 8cm lengths
8cm x 6cm lengths
Curl the long strip up to make four even rings, fasten with glue.
Follow the pattern for placing the double loops around the outer ring.
The method for sticking ends together and placing loops around the ring is identical to that for star A.

Star C

For the large inner ring:
Seven strips 5cm long
For the double loops:
Seven strips 8cm long

37

Seven strips 6cm long
Form rings from the 7cm x 5cm lengths of paper and glue together with small margins overlapping. Follow the method suggested in star A for forming the double loops.
Follow the diagram provided for placing the small rings and double loops around the large ring.

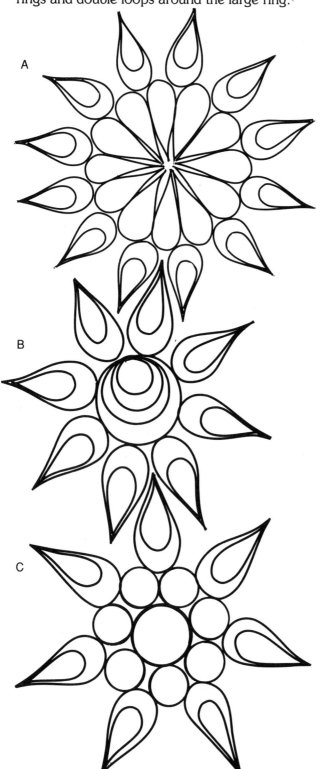

Bead baubles

Time: 🕐 *Skill:* ★

Requirements

Wooden beads, or beads of your choice:
Sixty beads for a large bauble
36 beads for a medium-size bauble
Eighteen beads for a small bauble
Florist's wire, or wire thin enough to thread through the beads and maintain its shape
Pliers, or suitably strong scissors
Thread for hanging

Method

Divide the beads evenly into three groups.
Thread them on to the wire.
Form into loops and gently twist the wire to hold the beads from slipping off. Allow a few millimetres of play between the beads.
To secure the round shape of the bauble, divide the beads evenly on the three "strings", and with a short piece of wire loop over the three wire strands and twist.
Tighten the long end of wire at the top of the bauble, and trim.
Pass the thread through the bauble and hang.
Variations: Hang a small bauble with a large one.
 Hang a small bauble below a large one.
 Experiment with other variations.
 Dry out pumpkin seeds, mealies or other seeds, and wire them instead of using beads.

Diagram for the construction of bead bauble

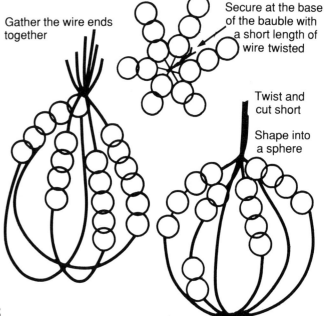

Gather the wire ends together

Secure at the base of the bauble with a short length of wire twisted

Twist and cut short

Shape into a sphere

Salt ceramics: hearts and stars

Time: Procedure takes place over several days.
Skill: ★

Requirements
One cup of flour
One cup of salt
About $\frac{1}{4}$ cup of water, and thereafter add water sparingly
Rolling pin or suitable wine bottle, mixing bowl
Thin cardboard templates of the heart and star
A sharp pointed knife
Drinking straw for making small holes
A baking tray
Poster-paint (red and yellow) and medium-sized paintbrush
String painted red and yellow to hang up the stars and hearts

Method
Mix the flour, salt and water in a mixing bowl to the consistency of a stiff dough.
Shake a film of flour on to a working surface.
Roll out the dough until it is 4mm thick.
Use the templates and a sharp knife to cut out the shapes.
Sprinkle a layer of flour on to the baking tray and place the shapes on it.
The shapes in the illustration are "baked" in a cool oven at 37°C over a period of two days. The shapes must be turned over from time to time to prevent the sides from curling up.
When the shapes have dried out, paint them red and yellow.
The drying period for this operation is about twelve hours.

Template for ceramic hearts and stars

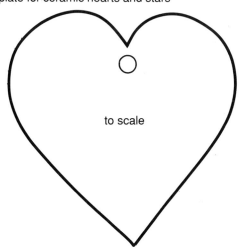

to scale

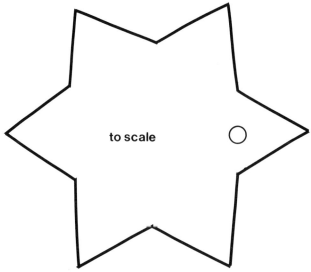

to scale

(**Tip**: once painted, hang the shapes up to dry hanging on a "pulled-open" wire paperclip. Hook these on to a raised baking rack).
Pass the string through the holes and hang up.

Ginger biscuits

Time: 🕐 *Skill*: ★

Requirements
Two cups of plain flour
$\frac{1}{2}$ cup moist brown sugar
One to two level teaspoons ground ginger
Pinch of salt
One level teaspoon baking powder
$\frac{1}{2}$ level teaspoon of bicarbonate of soda
$\frac{3}{8}$ cup of margarine or butter
$\frac{1}{4}$ cup of golden syrup
Circular pastry cutter, or cardboard template plus a sharp knife
Apple corer for making small holes
Red ribbon for hanging

Method
Sieve the dry ingredients well.
Cream the margarine or butter, sugar and syrup until light and soft.
Work in the dry ingredients and knead thoroughly.
Roll out the dough until about 5mm thick.
Cut into shapes. Use the apple corer to make a small hole. This should make about twelve to fifteen biscuits.
Place on a lightly-greased baking tray.
Bake in a hot oven (375°F) or 190°C for about 10-15 minutes.
Cool on the tray.
Allow to harden. Thread the ribbon through the holes and hang.

39

Glitzy lanterns

Time: 🕐 Skill: ★

Requirements
Lengths of 35mm photographic film
Scraps of glittering fabric
Lengths of yellow string, braid, wool or yarn
Large-eyed needle, scissors
Stationery punch for making holes (optional)

Method
Clean the film by soaking it in undiluted household bleach. Wear rubber gloves if possible, or at least keep your hand out of the fluid (work away from small children). Wash and dry.

Cut the film into lengths of 28cm and two of 8cm, the latter for the gusset.

Leave the first 4cm free, knot the yarn and stitch the gusset to the length of film. Complete the second edge in the same manner.

Poke the fragments of glittering fabric into the lantern, and make holes in the free ends of the film. Thread the yarn through the holes and hang.

Diagram for constructing a 'glitzy' lantern

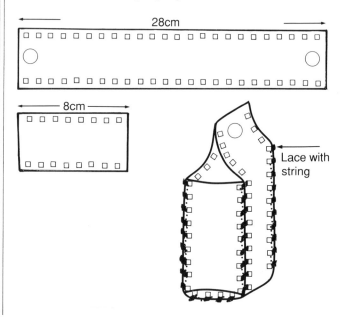

Lace with string

40

The angel, bell, star, dove, Christmas tree and heart

Time:  Skill: ★

Requirements

Scraps of fabric, red, green, yellow and Christmas-patterned fabrics, or other of your choice
Felt in red and black for the dove and angel
Short piece of braid trimming in red, yellow, green and white
Length of yellow yarn for the angel's hair
Short lengths of ribbon in green, red and yellow
Wadding (or other filling such as ruined pantihose cut-up finely)

Tracing paper, pencil
Needle, thread, scissors, pins (sewing-machine optional)
Bells
Beads for the star

Method

Trace the shapes and cut out.
Pin on to the fabric and cut out.
Stitch around the shape, leaving a section free to turn the shape inside out.
Stuff with filling.
Stitch up the hole.
Decorate with braid, felt, wool, bells, bows and beads according to your choice.
Stitch a length of cord in the appropriate place for hanging.

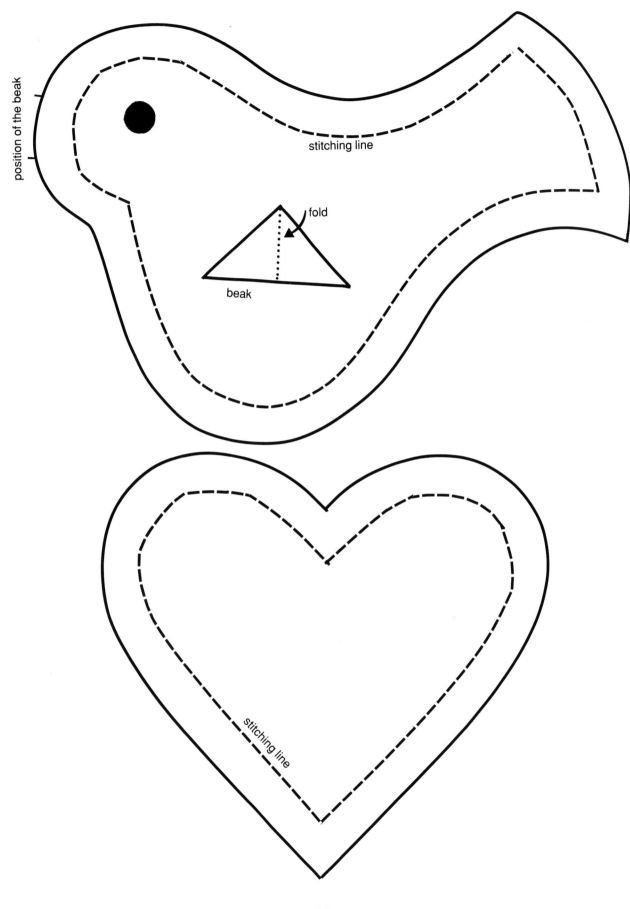

position of the beak

stitching line

fold

beak

stitching line

stitching line

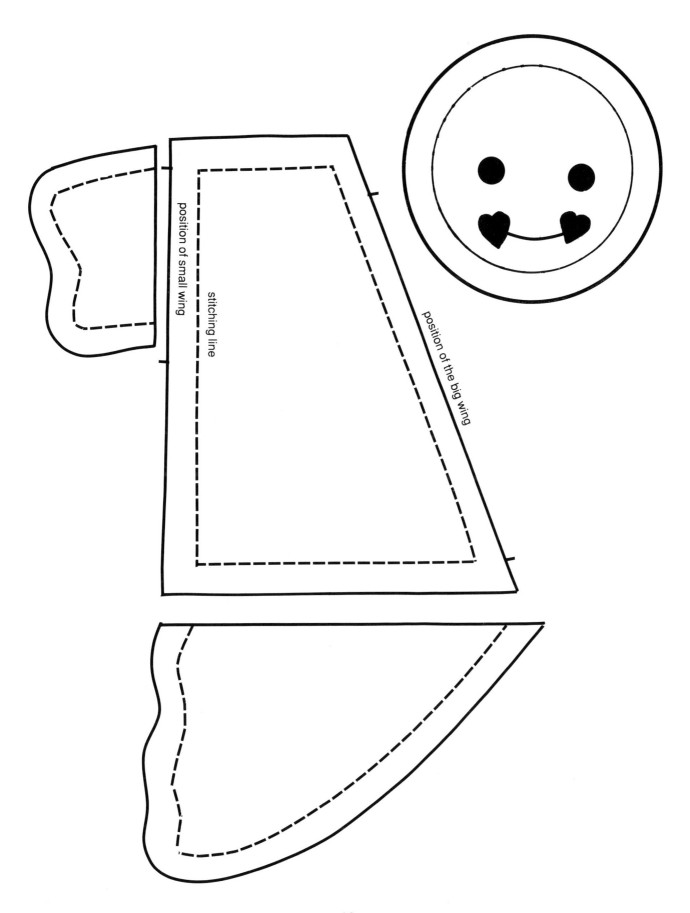

position of small wing

stitching line

position of the big wing

43

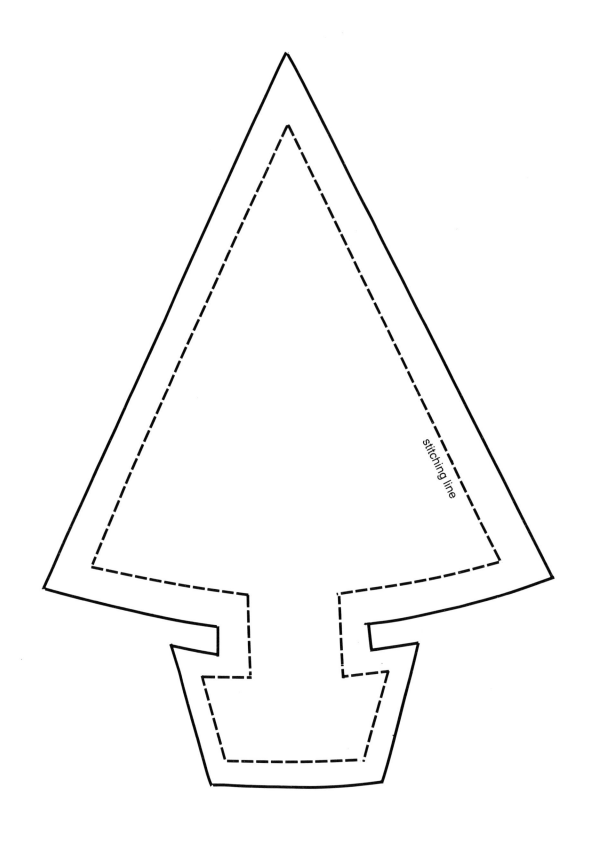

stitching line

44

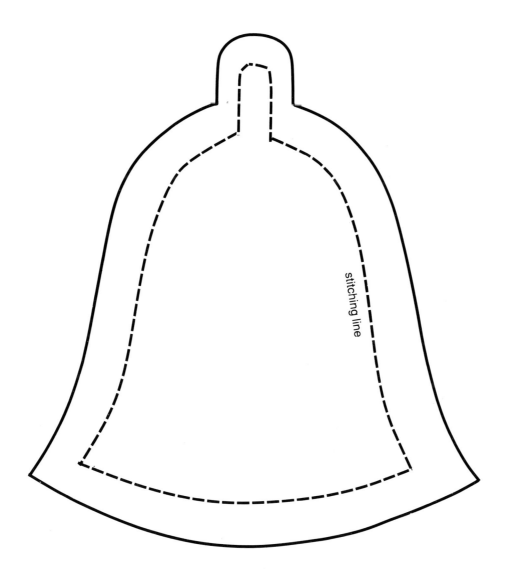

stitching line

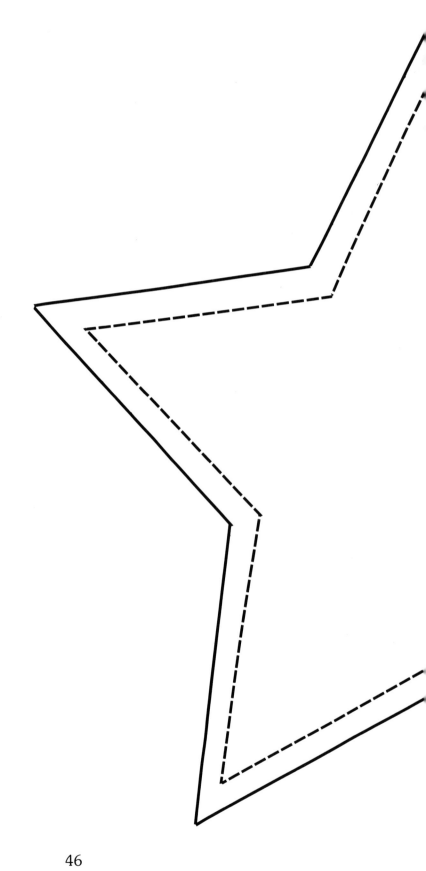

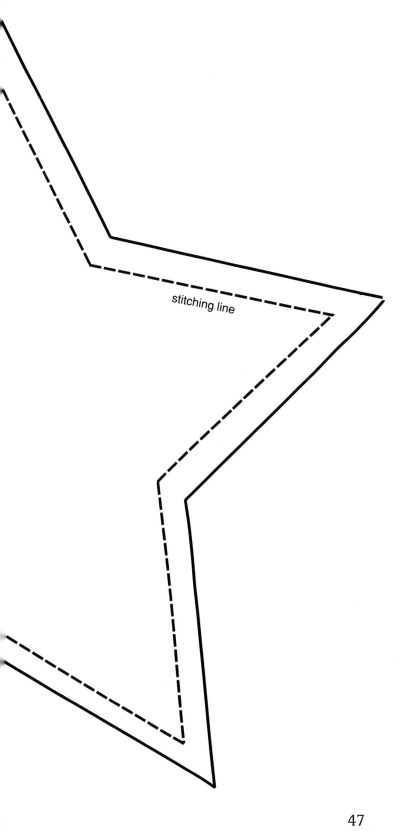

stitching line

6
The Christmas Card

Christmas cards

We all have friends and distant family members to whom we like to at least once a year say "I'm thinking of you". What better way to say it than with a Christmas card you have made yourself. This shows off your creative abilities and expresses the regard you have for special people.

The ideas presented here are quick methods of producing the most effective results. Once you are organised with a variety of coloured cards, pretty papers, poster- or water colour paints and glue, the process will not take long.

Important

Before you start, have a variety of different-sized envelopes beside you. There is *nothing* more frustrating than making a Christmas card, or any card for that matter, and not being able to find an envelope to fit! As you collect envelopes, bear in mind that there is a regulation size for standard mail. This is not smaller than 90mm x 140mm and not larger than 120mm x 235mm, not thicker than 5mm, and not more than 50g in mass.

Time: One clock – depending on design and method. Several cards can be made within an hour.
Skill: ★

Requirements

Stiff card in a variety of colours, with thin white paper to insert for messages in dark-coloured cards
Thin coloured plain and patterned paper, plastic film
Tracing paper, ruler, pencil, paintbrushes
Scissors, craft knife
Poster- or watercolour paints, fibre-tip pens, food colouring
Household bleach
Additional decoration of your choice

Method

Measure the envelope and make your double-folded card 6mm shorter in each direction. This ensures that the card will slip easily in and out of the envelope.

When cutting the card ensure that the corners are at right angles, so that your card will stand evenly.

Trace the designs of your choice on to tracing paper, and cut them out.

These are templates which you can use for many cards bearing the same design, such as the Christmas tree, Father Christmas, the doves, the star and the gift parcel.

Cut out the shape or shapes in coloured or patterned paper and paste on to the card you are making, or alternatively cut the shape out of the card and paste coloured or patterned paper behind it. This can be seen in several examples in the photograph.

Variations

1 Break away from rectangular cards by using the design for the triangular cards, such as Father Christmas, and the Christmas tree, and the irregular shape of the gift parcel.

2 Make cards of thin coloured art paper and "paint" designs on them with household bleach. Watch your designs appear; this is a fascinating technique.

3 Instead of using conventional paint use food colouring. If you do not have a paintbrush, wrap a piece of cotton wool around a thin stick and use it for the same purpose.

4 For some cards you do not need to go to any expense in purchasing coloured paper. Just tear coloured pages from old magazines and create images with torn pieces of paper glued to the surface of the card.

Once you start creating you will discover that the variety of techniques you can use are endless.

fold

51

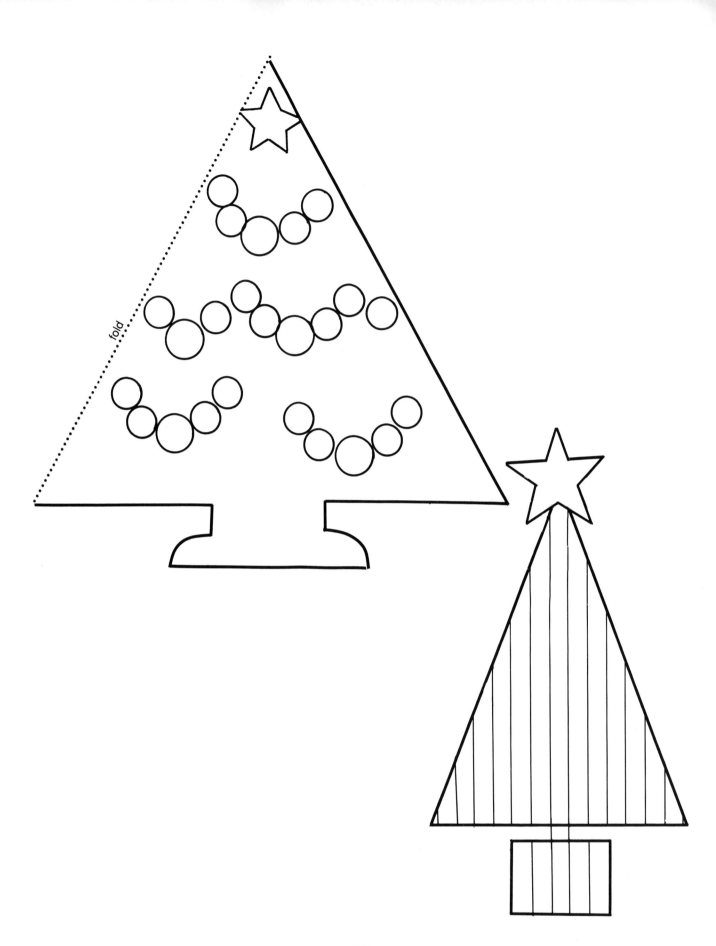

fold

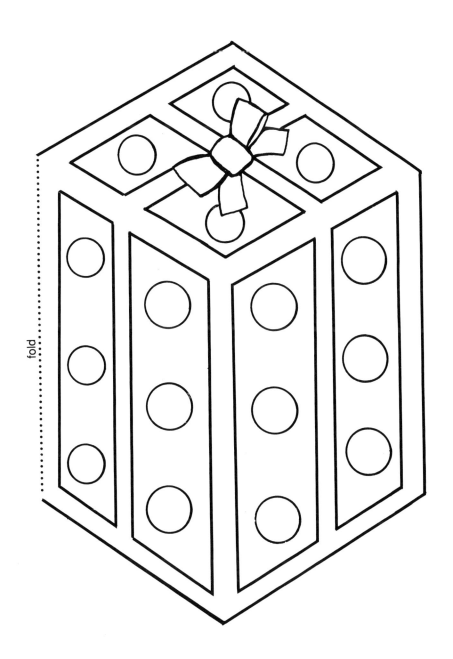

fold

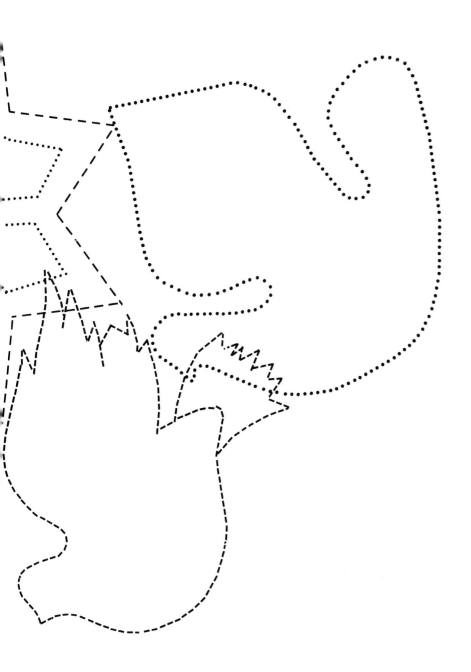

7
Gift
Wrapping

The sachet

Time:  Skill: ★

Requirements
Medium stiff cardboard, coloured or patterned
Thin decorated paper
Glue, and/or double-sided sticking tape
Tracing paper, pencil
Scissors, and a sharp craft knife

Method
The diagram provided may be copied for a small sachet, or enlarged by using either a photocopying machine with the enlarging mechanism, or by us-ing a grid system as demonstrated in diagram (b).

A further alternative is to scan the food freezing compartments of a supermarket to find a larger replica – enjoy the contents and use the package as a template.

Trace the design onto cardboard.

Cut out the shape.

With a sharp blade score (cut halfway through the paper) along the dotted lines, in order to bend the cardboard easily.

At this stage cover the cardboard with the decorated paper and glue down.

Glue the flap to the opposite side and allow to dry.

Bend the outer flaps inwards, paste tabs to the flaps if desired.

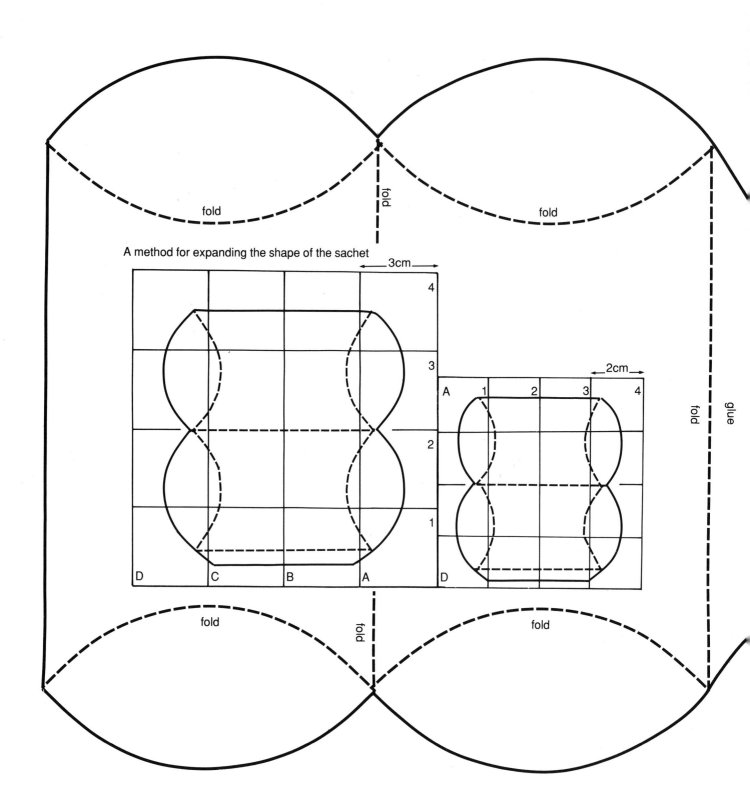

fold

fold

fold

A method for expanding the shape of the sachet

3cm

4

3

2

1

D   C   B   A

fold

2cm

A   1   2   3   4

D

fold

glue

fold

fold

fold

58

Paper packets

Time: 🕐 Skill: ★ ★

Requirements
Decorated or plain paper
Stiff paper or thinnest cardboard available
Double-sided sticking tape
Stationery punch (optional)
Decorated thread, string, ribbon
Tape measure or ruler, scissors and a craft knife

Method
Use a small book, such as a paperback, for the foundation shape.

Take a measurement around the circumference of the book and allow an extra 2cm for the overlap.

Take a second measurement from top to bottom, allowing 2cm to 3cm at the top for an overlap, and $\frac{3}{4}$ of the width of the book for the base of the packet.

Cut out the shape.

Cut a strip of thin cardboard, 2cm to 3cm wide and the length of the paper.

With the decorated surface face down, glue the strip of thin cardboard to the top of the paper, fold over and press down firmly.

Wrap the decorated paper around the book and with the double-sided sticking tape glue the overlap down.

Fold the base by first pressing down the upper overlap; secondly, fold the two corners towards the centre, and finally place a strip of double-sided sticking tape on the bottom flap and fold over the upper flap and press down firmly.

Before removing the book, run your thumb and first finger over the folds to secure the shape. Punch holes in the top edge, pull decorative cords through them and tie.

Tip: Decorated cords can be made on the zigzag sewing-machine by using the widest zigzag and the longest straight stitch settings.

Colourful threads are stitched over two or three strands of wool, yarn or thin ribbon.

Two or three layers of threads on top of each other make interesting cords for tying purposes.

Diagram for the construction of paper packets

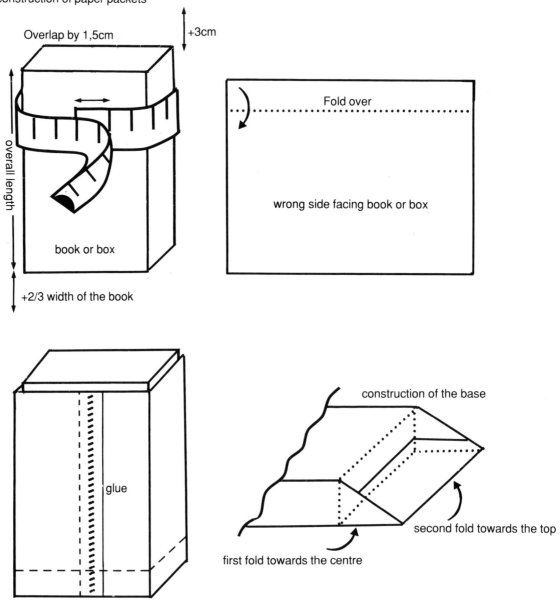

Overlap by 1,5cm

+3cm

overall length

book or box

+2/3 width of the book

Fold over

wrong side facing book or box

glue

construction of the base

second fold towards the top

first fold towards the centre

Wrap the paper around the book or the box

Decorate your own wrapping paper

Wrapping paper can be costly; effectively decorated paper can be achieved with minimal requirements that can be found around your home, such as poster-paint, left-over dyes from dyeing clothes, coloured ink or even food colouring and household bleach.
You will need:

 Thick and thin paintbrushes
 Sheets of thin white paper

Method

For creating your own designs, use any of the colouring agents suggested above.
To create a blotched effect: fully cover a sheet of paper with mixed dye or ink. When it is dry, flick household bleach over the paper with a thin brush and allow to dry.

Another suggestion is to use brown wrapping paper and glue pictures to the surface. This can be particularly attractive if old Christmas wrapping paper is used.
Have you ever thought of using black garbage bags or colourful shelf paper for wrapping? Leave the garbage bags to air for few days to get rid of the strange smell they have.
Wrap your gifts in the manner described on page 62.
One of the gifts in the photograph is decorated with a frieze of Christmas trees cut out of red plastic sheeting. You can use red fabric or paper to do the same (see diagram).
A red bow is tied around the circumference.

Variation

Further decorative elements added are gold paper doilies and flat bows which are made from strips of florist's ribbon trimmed to a point and stuck down.

Diagram for cutting a length of Christmas trees

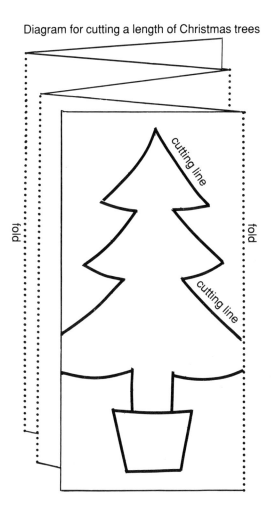

Wrapping a gift

Time: 🕐 *Skill:* ★

Requirements
Decorated paper
Scissors, a craft knife
Double-sided sticking tape, general purpose/transparent sticking tape
Tape measure, ruler
Bow, ribbons of your choice

Method
Beautifully-wrapped gifts need not entail vast expense. All you need is a tidy, careful and loving manner of wrapping up a gift.
The choice of the right paper, ribbons, or other decorative material, is of considerable importance.
Measure the length and depth of your gift.
Measure the circumference of the gift, allowing a 2cm to 3cm overlap.
Cut out the shape carefully, ensuring straight edges and square corners, especially if you are covering a box-like shape.
Fold over 1,5cm of the overlap for which you have made allowance.
Fold over the gift and secure the overlap with a thin strip of double-sided sticking tape.
When working with the sides, press the flaps towards the centre and press the paper along the diagonal fold.
Fold the upper flap inwards, bring the lower flap over the upper one, and secure with small pieces of double-sided sticking tape.
Make sure that this is neatly done.

Folds and pleats on wrapping paper

There is particular enjoyment in decorating a gift. Some effects can be achieved with minimal effort and expense.

Method
Measure the length, breadth or circumference of the gift.
With this in mind, add about 15cm to 20cm, and cut the paper.
Roll it into a thin tube, keeping the edges even.
Flatten the roll with the palm of your hand.
Unfurl the paper and find the central ridges.
Fold into pleats away from the centre, keeping the folds parallel.
Press the pleats down.
At this stage the pleats can be further decorated by slotting in decorated ribbon, paper, fabric, or stitching them with the sewing-machine.
Hold the pleats together with sticking tape at the back.
Carefully attach this to your gift.

Variation

Pleated paper can be placed at an angle instead of lengthwise or breadthwise.
Try using two tones of coloured paper, or perhaps contrasting colours.

8
The Decorated Table

Table decorations

With special thanks to Gretchen Reich (flowers)

"Transparent" dome with a pink candle

Time: *Skill:*

Requirements:
Cardboard or thick cartridge paper for the star, about 50cm square
Aluminium foil: expose the glossy surface
Scissors, ruler, pencil, compass
Newspaper
Clear plastic for bows (suggestion: Use plastic bags.)
Florist's wire or thin hairpins
Flower foam (oasis)
Silver (or home-made silvered) pipe-cleaners

Method
Cut out a 4cm deep block of flower foam for the core of the arrangement.
Wrap the flower foam in a piece of foil.
To make the plastic bows:
Take several layers of clear plastic, about 15cm square.
Bunch together in the middle, twist and pin to the foam with a loop of florist's wire or the thin hairpins.
A large number of such bows will be needed to surround the foam block.
Finally fluff each bow out and complete the dome shape by trimming.
Add the final decorative elements, such as the silver pipe-cleaners. These are available from the florist's supply shop. To make your own, dip the pipe-cleaner into glue and cover it with silver glitter.
To obtain the corkscrew effect, wrap the pipe-cleaner around a pencil.
The illustration shows the dome decorated with dried and dyed "bunny-tails". Perhaps these are not available in your area: you can use dried flowers and grasses as alternatives.

To add further interest to the arrangement, insert short lengths of silver tinsel and silver baubles. Place a candle in the centre of the dome.

The large star

The large star is made of thick cartridge paper, covered with foil with the glossy side exposed. First make a template (shape) of newspaper 50cm square.

1 Fold the square in half.
2 Establish the centre of the rectangle (a).
3 To avoid confusion, mark the A to E points around the rectangle back and front, following the diagram.
4 Fold A - a across a - C.
5 Fold a - B over on to a - E.
6 Fold a - D over on to a - C.
7 Cut along the dotted line.

This is known as the "one-cut" star, and is sufficiently accurate for the table decoration. Should you wish to construct a perfect five-pointed star, draw a circle with the aid of a compass, mark off 72° at five intervals around the circumference with the aid of a protractor. Join the points with the aid of a ruler, and cut out.

Diagram to make a 'one cut' star

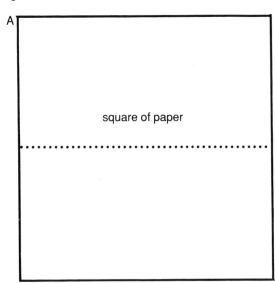

square of paper

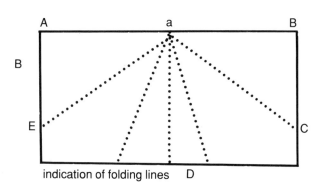

indication of folding lines

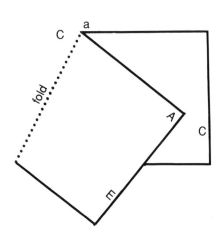

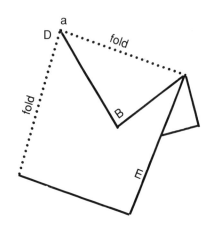

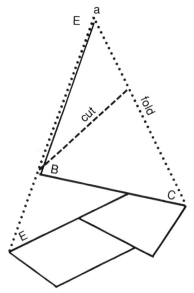

66

Red Christmas cracker

Time:  Skill:

Requirements
One metre of red net – length 150cm
Flower foam (oasis)
Aluminium foil
Small container such as a margarine tub
About twenty red carnations or red flowers of your choice
Semi-stiff cardboard about 15cm square
Red fabric, paper or poster-paint to disguise the cardboard
Scissors
Red ribbon or string

Method
The Christmas cracker is made by folding the net in half and then in half again, i.e. four layers.
Roughly gather the net and roughly divide into thirds. At these two points bind loosely with string or ribbon.

Place soaked flower foam in the tub.
Wrap the red-surfaced cardboard around the tub and place within the centre of the cracker, ensuring that the net is drawn up the sides of the red cardboard covering.
Bind the two "necks" of the net cracker as close as possible to the tub, and fluff out the ends of the cracker.
Arrange the flowers according to the design or in a manner of your own choice.
Keep the flower foam moist so as to keep the flowers fresh.

Diagram for constructing the red flower Christmas cracker

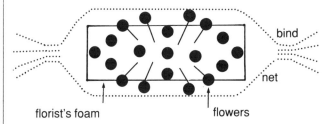

Christmas tree of daisies

Time: 🕐🕐 Skill: ★

Requirements

Flower foam (oasis)
Silver tinsel – about two lengths
Daisies, or white flowers of your choice
Aluminium foil
Florist's wire or thin hairpins
Small discarded food container in tin or plastic, about 2,5cm high
Scissors, a sharp knife

Method

For the "core" of the "tree" cut a flower foam block in half and slightly taper one of the halves at the top to resemble a cone.
Soak the foam in water.
First arrange a line of daisies in a spiral formation from top to bottom.

Important: do not pre-cut the tinsel, as each length will vary.
On either side of the daisy line, pin a strand of tinsel down at the top with either florist's wire or a

Diagram for constructing the daisy Christmas tree

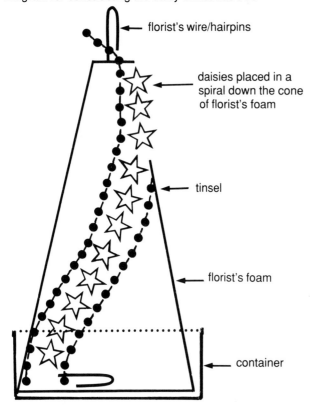

← florist's wire/hairpins

daisies placed in a spiral down the cone of florist's foam

← tinsel

← florist's foam

← container

hairpin. Closely follow the line of flowers to the bottom.
Arrange a further line of daisies on either side of the tinsel.
Continue in this manner until the foam has been covered.
Place the daisy tree into the small container which has been covered with foil.
Keep the flower foam moist to keep the daisies looking their best.

Christmas crackers

Time: 🕐 Skill: ★

Requirements

Crêpe paper
Thin paper for lining
Thin cardboard for stiffening the central area
Two cracker forms, one large (roller towel tube) one short (toilet paper tube)
Scissors, craft knife, ruler, pencil
Glue
Piece of string – about a metre long
Exterior decoration, small pictures, gold, silver, white doilies
Inside fillers: bangers available at a shop selling fireworks or at a toy shop
Mottoes, small gifts, paper hats

Method

Cut pieces of crêpe paper with the crêpe running parallel to the longer edge, measuring 30,5cm x 16cm. Frill the edges.
Cut pieces of lining paper measuring 28cm x 15cm.
Cut pieces of stiffening cardboard measuring 15cm x 9cm.
Place the papers and cardboard in the following order:
crêpe paper, lining paper, a banger, thin cardboard.
Place dabs of glue along the exposed edge of the crêpe paper and roll around the long form.
When the glue is dry enough, pull the large form back to meet the edge of the stiffening cardboard, and insert the small form to meet the large one. Allow for a small intervening margin of 0,5cm. This you will have to feel with your fingers.

Tie the string to the leg of the table or chair on which you are sitting.

With the length of string in your hand, wind it around the 0,5cm area between the two cardboard tubes and gently "choke" the cracker.

Hold the string in place for a short period to ensure that the "neck" remains, then remove the string.

Pull out the short tube.

Before removing the long tube to the area beyond the stiffening cardboard, insert the mottoes, gifts and hats.

With the larger tube in place, repeat the same performance of "choking" the cracker.

Complete the cracker by adding the decoration of your choice.

Variation

If you do not have crêpe paper, try using one sheet of a paper napkin. Your table decorations will look that much more exclusive by having table napkins and crackers to match.

References

Enoler C, Johnson N, Walter G. *The Decorated Tree*. New York: Abrams, 1982.

Hadfield M, Hadfield J. *The Twelve Days of Christmas*. London: Cassel, 1961.

Muir F, Muir J. *A Treasury of Christmas. Stories, Traditions and Pastimes of the Christmas Festival*. London: Robinson Books, 1981.